Empower Your Daily Thoughts

1

Word Wonders

31 Days
Abounding Towards Power To Transfer In Your Daily Life!

Parice C Parker

Word Wonders

Wonder why the world is gaining more than you?

Empower Your Daily Thoughts

Published by Fountain of Life Publisher's House

P. O. Box 922612 Norcross, GA 30010
Phone: 404-936-3989
Please Email Manuscripts to: publish@pariceparker.biz
For all book orders including wholesale email: sales@pariceparker.biz
To request author email: author@pariceparker.biz
www.pariceparker.biz

Fountain of Life Publishing House is committed to excellence in the publishing industry. The Company reflects the philosophy established by the founder, based on Psalm 68:11, *"The Lord gave the word and great was the company of those who published it."*

Book design copyright © 2016 by Parice C Parker. All rights reserved.
Cover Design by Parice C. Parker
Interior design by Parice C. Parker
Editor: FOLPH Editor's Team

Published in the United States of America

ISBN: 9780978716271
3.23.2016 Revised

Word Wonders

Table of Contents

Empower Your Daily Thoughts

Introduction

There is only one way to gain righteously. You must believe in the WORD. Too many put all their trust in religion and not near enough in the WORD. It works, even when you can't. It will move mountains, alter your season and prosper you. However, you need right now faith. You need to trust this WORD more than you trust yourself. The WORD does not have an option of letting you down, it just works! I know this WORD has more love capability for you than you do for yourself. Just, trust in this WORD.

Right now your faith has the possibility to produce whatever you need, want or desire. Think of it as past tense. Though your eyes can not see it in the natural, glimpse it in the supernatural. If you can perceive it, then it is yours right now. It is your faith, which is going to bring forth evidence in your life. Faith defines your trust in The Most High. What is your faith producing? How do others view you and what is your faith speaking?

Faith production works as an assembly line in a warehouse. Furthermore, heaven is your stock dealer. It is your belief that calculates your faith, and the more you believe in the WORD that cranks it up. Once you can believe in the impossible, your hope will cause you to endure. As you communicate with your hope, it inspires your faith to bring forth your essence. Let your desire influence your belief. Right now it may not look possible; that's faith. Believing in the unseen, but hoping for all of your impossibilities to come to pass. Your faith is more influential than money, doctors, lawyers or anything else dominant. Your faith will produce the impossible. Hire your faith to produce your substance or whatever you need and your hope to show forth evidence. Trust matters, and if you don't have it, do not look for anything. Your faith is what delivers; it is your Supernatural Post Master.

Hebrews 11:1
NOW faith is the substance of things hoped for, the evidence of things not seen.

Preface
What Inspired Word Wonders

The WORD has blessed my life enormously, and Jesus wants me to share it with you. Come and explore the powers of His WORD with me. Perhaps, you can share your daily devotion with as many as He allows. Someone other than you needs a WORD Today.

A lot of the writings He instructs me to share are one on one experiences. I had to endure in the WORD. I realize that I was truly chosen to explore His WORD so that others will receive more authority in their lives. I use to think I was cursed because I have gone through the fire over and over. Save for Jesus, continues to prove Himself to me. Then I noticed, that I was blessed and highly favored. This is my first daily devotional book, which was requested by a friendly neighbor. God speaks through people, listen to your next steps. I pray that this little book brings forth great clout in your life.

I love to write small books. My goal is to produce more readers to gain understandings of the WORD. Knowledge is authoritative, and many take it for granted. The more you read, the more knowledge you will gain. Let's free our spirit through the WORD. This little book has hidden potential, to renovate your life. Don't forget to share it throughout the entire day.

May today be more blessed, than yesterday.

Word Wonders

Day One
Put God First

Always put God first in your day, He loves it. When someone takes the time to think of me, it causes me to have a better day. It is not a good feeling when people forget about you or put you last on their list. God is a jealous God. He wants love too! Only because we cannot see, touch, or feel Him every day as a living human being does not excuse excluding Him. Most people, when they wake up in the morning, go to the restroom, brush their teeth and wash their face. Always, ripping and rushing their morning start. Most of them push the snooze button on their alarm clock, dreading getting out of bed. We should be glad that we wake up. Be excited and joyous about your new day; after all, you will never be able to relive it again. So do not take another minute of your life for granted. Tremendous joy should be our everyday start, bursting with zeal. Happy that we still have life and another opportunity to get our life right, as well as accomplish more goals. He loves it when we put Him first; it makes Him feel a part of you. Just remember, to put God first. There is no better way to start your day!

My Daily Word

> Matthew 6:33
> But seek ye first the kingdom of God, and his righteousness; and all these things shall be added unto you.

This word instructs us to seek the kingdom first. Get to know His Word. Begin to look forward starting your day with the WORD. It is the best way I know to start a day, because before it is over you may have needed that particular Word for something in your life. God may have you sharing it with many throughout the day. Many people are in such a hurry in the morning, and they only forget to recognize our Heavenly Father. Can you imagine how it feels to be ignored or not thought of at all? That is how many allow God to feel every day, as though He is not important or a part of their lives. There is only one true way to get to know Him, and it is through the WORD. (John 1:1). And after you seek Him in the WORD, seek after righteousness. Throughout your day make the right decisions. Remember; there will be consequences. Do what is right. Put this scripture to work early in the morning, every day for the rest of your life and you will have no regrets. Because soon afterward, there is a promise that will follow and only The Almighty has the power to give you all things.

Share this daily WORD.

Matthew 24:35
**Heaven and earth shall pass away, but my words
shall not pass away.**

Word Wonders

Day Two
He Wants Love Too

For many years, I thought as long as I prayed every morning and went to church some Sundays that I was showing God, love. That was far from the attention He wanted from me. One weekend I was feeling so lonely and empty inside. I took a ride out of town. I went to visit one of my aunts. My uncle was sharing this WORD with us; it instantly gave me a new since of hope. It changed my life forever. As He read this scripture (Proverbs 8:17), I immediately felt better. I know God had me to travel from Charlotte to Atlanta just for me to receive this WORD at a dinner table. I felt so loved by Him, instantly He stroked my heart and put a spirit of calmness inside. Know that if you ever need love, that He is waiting. Man can not nearly love you as you desire to be loved. What is life, when you feel unloved? It hurts, and it is lonely. He is ready early in the morning in the making for your day to love Him. From that day forward I begin to seek Him first because I had to prove that I loved Him too.

My Daily Word

> *Proverbs 8:17*
> *I love them that love me; and those that seek me early shall find me.*

Remembers when you were in the dating game, and you met someone you were not attracted. You avoided their calls, and you did not want to respond. Many let God feel that very same way as they continually avoid His love daily. It is no fun feeling alone, not loved, or cheated. It makes you feel unworthy, and not attracted. I tell Him every day that I love Him. Fascinate Him, with they way you show Him love and watch how He mesmerizes you.

Share this daily WORD.

Matthew 24:35
Heaven and earth shall pass away, but my words shall not pass away.

Word Wonders

Day Three
Abundant Blessings

Only what you do for the sake of righteousness, is going to last. Have you ever brought cheap trash bags and they break to you? When you need them the most, they will let you down every time. God will never let you down. I used the trash bags for an example because many can relate to cheap products. If you invest quality time in the WORD, you will reap things that will be everlasting and durable. Building a daily personal relationship with the WORD is the greatest thing you will ever do. The WORD has the power to instruct the truth, deep in you and change the way you trust Him. Do not allow the WORD to be emptied out of your life, heart and mind. Because you will only be cheating you out of living the best life ever. I tell people, live the best life you can because you will only get one.

My Daily Word

> *Proverbs 8:18*
> *Riches and honors are with me; yea, durable riches and righteousness.*

Many search for love in all the wrong places. All the love, things and blessing that one will ever need is with The Most High. He has the power to give you good things that money can not buy. Just love Him right. His WORD is very powerful. The enemy trick many with all sorts of other treats just to separate them from the truth. When more people strike into the truth of serving Jesus whole heartedly, they will gain a guaranteed life of tremendous love and blessings. Plus, these blessings will make your cup run over. Abundant blessings are what He is known for and they are durable, as well as everlasting!

Share this daily WORD.

Matthew 24:35
**Heaven and earth shall pass away, but my words
shall not pass away.**

Word Wonders

Day Four
Admirable Permit

Our Heavenly Father only gives the best quality of life, and He will lead you into a life worth living that will become priceless. Everything is not always summed up with a monetary value. He gives the most impressive gifts, things, stuff and others not made bu mans hands. Somethings are not able to be compared with any worldly gift which is Divine Wisdom. Nothing is finer than His Wisdom. The most excellent choice you could make every day is to permit Him the tribute in making your life admirable. When you think He is not there, He is. When you think nothing is working out, He has already worked it out. It's just a matter of time when it takes place. I will never forget. I needed an emergency, and I was was talking to my aunt. She said, "Darling I don't care what you need or the size of your miracle. God is an on time God, and if you need it by 12 midnight, He will show up by 11:59 PM because He is never late."

My Daily Word

> Proverbs 8:19
> My fruit is better than gold, yea, than fine gold; and my revenue than choice silver.

There is nothing equivalent to Him. His fruit produces more value than gold ever will. I am talking about the highest quality of life, live, peace and having a sound mind. Nothing in this world is more worthy and more powerful. You will reap unheard of benefits, as long as you put the WORD first in your life. I can never put into words how much value His WORD will bring you. However, I can guarantee you that you will be far better off than you are now! Just begin to study the WORD every day for yourself and the WORD will soon gain your trust. His WORD will start to become fruitful in your life, sweet and tasty. Oh taste, and see how sweet He is.

Share this daily WORD.

Matthew 24:35
Heaven and earth shall pass away, but my words shall not pass away.

Word Wonders

Day Five
Life Instructor

The Almighty is our life instructor, as long as we are on the right path. It is just like you are in the presence of a loving mother and she leads you by the hand. Loving parents see their children. They are very protective. A loving mother will greatly sacrifice for the needs of her children. She will do what no one else will. Jesus is the same way. He leads us out of harms way and guides us into His truth. That is the way He prepares us to receive favor. Also, as long as you listen to you will obtain His blessings.

My Daily Word

> *Proverbs 8:20*
> *I lead in the way of righteousness, in the midst of the paths of judgment:*

Though your situation may not always appear healthy, Jesus is there. While others are judging you, God is leading you. Yes, sometimes your wrong will cause you to step into righteousness, and put claims on your life. It happened to me. Jesus is very powerful. He can do what He wants, and when He is ready. Remember, He is in the midst, regardless of your circumstance. Do not allow what your eyes are seeing deter your faith! However, allow it to make you become wiser as well as a greater believer! He is only doing this because He loves you, and when it is all over, you too will agree.

Share this daily WORD.

Matthew 24:35
Heaven and earth shall pass away, but my words shall not pass away.

Word Wonders

Day Six
Vision Expansion

Once you begin to explore His WORD for yourself, and He will start leading you to great vision. Things you only dreamed of, He will give you and more. Many things will be revealed to you, through your determination. As God notices your ability, He will give you treasures and the aptitude to obtain considerable substance. All He is waiting on is love. He wants you to love Him.

My Daily Word

> *Proverbs 8:21*
> *That I may cause those that love me to inherit substance;*
> *and I will fill their treasures.*

Have you ever gained something and lost it? Men seek wealth, fame and fortune; things that are made by man. Once you begin to find things not man-made, such as The Most High. He will start to fill you with a vision that will cause you to inherit a considerable substance. Many spend a lifetime searching for money and still can not obtain it. He will teach you all things and give you the vision to cause your substance to overflow. I do not know a greater vision writer and vision instructor than He. With the WORD, Jesus will give you guidance to maintain your possessions, integrity, wealth and riches. Plus, you will operate in a spirit of humbleness as He begins to fill your treasures supernaturally.

Empower Your Daily Thoughts

Share this daily WORD.

Matthew 24:35
Heaven and earth shall pass away, but my words shall not pass away.

Word Wonders

Day Seven
Everyday Decisions

When I could not depend on anyone else, Jesus was there. He has provided evidence of His love over, and over again in my life. No other has done some great things in my life, like Jesus. I want the whole world to know I serve a Savior that will save you in any circumstance, condition, and situation. All you need is to seek Him early and explore the favor of righteous. He will allow supernatural favor in your life. Daily I send out a WORD to cover, and protect my family as well as bring goodness into my life. That is why I can rightfully include Him in my early morning prayers, and everyday decisions. Make sure you establish the WORD daily in your heart.

My Daily Word

Isaiah 54:11
So shall my word be that goeth forth out of my mouth: it shall not return unto me void, but it shall accomplish that which I please, and it shall prosper in the thing whereto I sent it.

Your daily decisions help plan your future.

Let the WORD deliver your needs. The WORD is potent; it has a command to do just what it says. Let the WORD build your faith. Send a daily WORD out before you, and watch how Jesus will be your strengthen you to accomplish substantially. Quite naturally we may fail at many things in life, but the WORD can not fail us! Where ever you send a WORD, there it may be fulfilled. However, if you do not send a WORD, then how can it accomplish your needs? It is extremely necessary to send a WORD out before your day. So, therefore, it can acquire your needs, and perform its task for your life. Through the WORD are your peace and comfort. Try it, and don't leave home without it.

29

Share this daily WORD.

Matthew 24:35
Heaven and earth shall pass away, but my words shall not pass away.

Word Wonders

Day Eight
Learn to Listen

Often we do not listen; that is the biggest mistake we all have made. But the greatest life changer is when you pay attention. Our Heavenly Father speaks to us, through life situations, conditions, and circumstances. All along He gives us instruction, but do we listen? Yes, many hear. Although they do not want to obey, listen, or pay attention, because He is speaking to you.

My Daily Word

Proverbs 8:33
Hear instruction, and be wise, and refuse it not.

Often God speaks to us, and we are too busy to hear Him. Well, that is what many do to the voice of God, blot Him out. There is so much going on in many lives a lot of people refuse instruction. Every time He speaks, it is for us to gain WISDOM. With intelligence, you will have no lack. Begin to find a quiet place or area, and prepare yourself to hear Him. Pray and ask Him to speak to you. Also, let Him know to make His voice clear so that you will receive insight and obtain true understanding. I always pray or ask for a specific thing to let me know that He has spoken or answered me. It is okay to ask Him to answer you, and to let you know that it was Him. Sometimes we are listening but to the wrong voice. Other times we think we did not hear correctly, especially when things are not going right in our lives.

Share this daily WORD.

Matthew 24:35
Heaven and earth shall pass away, but my words shall not pass away.

Word Wonders

Day Nine
Prep Yourself

Where ever I can receive a good WORD, I want to be. Preparation gets you ready for what is coming. I do not know what your something is, but you do. God wants to prepare you for greater because He has more for you. Not merely just things, but wisdom. If you ever want something to seek Him, He is the Master Planner. After all, He has all your needs, and heart desires and they are awaiting you!

My Daily Word

> *Proverbs 8:34*
> *Blessed is the man that heareth me, watching daily at my gates, waiting at the post of my doors.*

If I listen to The Most High, I am going to be blessed? That is what His WORD clearly says. Many try and sow seeds for a blessing. Yea, surely they come. Nevertheless, aren't you tired of those quick fixes? Every day favor is guaranteed, when one listens. Read this scripture, meditate on it day and night. Allow it marinate in your heart, until it enters your soul.

Share this daily WORD.

Matthew 24:35
Heaven and earth shall pass away, but my words shall not pass away.

Word Wonders

Day Ten
Beware of Whose Beside You

The way He cares for us, proves His love. Make sure you check to see if He need something. Daily, He will say yes. He needs us to represent Him well, and to be respectful of everyone we come in contact. In the way we love, will show others who we serve. Our Heavenly Father has needs just as we do. Perhaps, many will want to fall in love with Him after they see your love for Him. Have you ever been in a public place, and saw children being disrespectful and mischievous? Well, that is exactly how believers misrepresent our HEAVENLY FATHER. Many do not realize how they cause others to be wrongfully misled through their mischievous acts. People are paying attention to how you represent Jesus.

I will never forget, one day I went up to some teenagers, and I introduced myself. I waited for them to finish speaking, and they were obscene to me when they ignored my presence. Nevertheless, they were talking about their church activities, and the first thought is I would not want to be a part of them. A lot of people have been wrongly misled because of believers' actions. Beware, who is in your presence, because it could be a Messiah seeker. Also, if ignored or you are rude. It could cost you an opportunity

37

to spread salvation. Remember your reason for being a believer, and keep in mind why you are one. Eight five percent of the time a soul will be standing next to you, and God would not want you to ignore them.

My Daily Word

> *Proverbs 8:35*
> *For whoso findeth me findeth life, and shall obtain favor of the LORD.*

Whoever searches the heart of His WORD, receives favor. His desire from the beginning of times is for us to love personally, and know Him. He wants you also to desire to Him. Jesus is everything to me, and without Him I am nothing. He has proved not only that His WORD is true, but that His loved is unconditional. I love the way He loves me, and I would not trade His love for anything.

Share this daily WORD.

Matthew 24:35
Heaven and earth shall pass away, but my words shall not pass away.

Ponder on This WORD

> **Matthew 16:19**
> **And I will give unto thee the keys of the kingdom of heaven: and whatsoever thou shalt bind on earth shall be bound in heaven: and whatsoever thou shalt loose on earth shall be loosed in heaven.**

Once you know of all His saving power, no one will be able to convince you that He is not your Savior. I know Him as my Healer, Deliverer and my Life Protector. I testify, even before anyone asks. I know who He is in my life. Once He reveals Himself to you, there will be no devil in hell to stop you. You will be able to stand when you want to fall, because you will have assurance in His WORD. When trouble comes you will stand on His WORD, because trouble has no power compared to His WORD. When nothing else in my life worked, He Did. I was able to stand as He held me up. He is The Rock of my SALVATION! I was able to prevail as He gave me power. Also, I trusted in Jesus. I know that whatever I loosed, and bind on earth, that Jesus was binding it and loosing in Heaven. Plus, I walked in agreement with the WORD.

The enemies do not want people to know Him in that manner because Releasing KINGDOM Authority in their lives. They will not look at their unfortunate situations and give in. When I was not bold in the WORD, I fell. Many things tried to conquer me. But, when I grew up in the WORD I was able to stand and not be moved. I begin to

41

speak strongly because I had the WORD to back me up. I was no longer afraid. It is time to stand. Know what you are standing on, a True Foundation. David stood, Moses stood, and so did many others. They stood on The Solid Rock.

As you begin to stand on The Rock, there will be no turning back. Nothing can come between you and Him because He will be substantial enough to hold you, and all your burdens will be released. You will know where your trust is, where your help comes from and your confidence. He is my way maker in the midnight hour and peace in the middle of a storm. He is everything I need and not a second too late. He is always on time! Who do you say Jesus is to you? Tell somebody.

Word Wonders

Day Eleven
Words of Wisdom

A righteous person will always give you words of wisdom. Every time they speak, a well of life will spring forth out of their mouth. Once you receive the words of wisdom, you will gain a fresh new hope because now you clearly understands. So, therefore, speak life to others, and encourage one another. It will only come back to you from another source. Whatever you sow that too shall you reap.

My Daily Word

Proverbs 10:11
The mouth of a righteous man is a well of life: but violence coverth the mouth of the wicked.

Surely you have been in the company of negative people. They will drain your hope. It is not okay for any good man to be in the company of a wicked minded person, especially if they are not strong. Now I am not talking about you should never help them occasionally or give them a good word of counsel. But if they are not transforming into goodness, they are not right for you to be around. A good man speaks life, and it is enough that could change a generation. Once you receive a well of life, it will transform your life and change the way you think well as carry yourself. You will know how to maintain that well that flows out of you. Goodness will continuously flow through you, good words of recommendation, good deeds and you to will become a well of life for another. Remember, overflow in goodness so that someone else can be filled with a well of goodness.

Share this daily WORD.

Mark 13:31
Heaven and earth shall pass away: but my words shall not pass away.

Word Wonders

Day Twelve
Astonishing

When God first started enhancing my faith. He astonished me! I saw things that many thought I was just dreaming. Perhaps, they thought I had gone over the edge. Although, He made my impossibilities all promising. It was the muscle of anticipation that encouraged me. Many did not believe that it was possible, but I did. God gave me the vision to make my hope come alive and gave birth to others hopeless dream.

My Daily Word

> *Psalms 40:2*
> *He brought me up out of a horrible pit, out of the miry clay, and set my feet upon a rock, and established my goings.*

If it had not been for my horrible pit stops. I would not be where I am today. When I was in a horrible pit after horrible pit. He led me towards righteousness. Though I thought I was already on the right path towards a good, life. I was not there yet. Although when He finished altering my course of life. He set me well on my way. He delivered me on the ROCK. After I begin seeking His face daily through the word. He established my going,s and ordered my steps. Once He establishes you, there is no turning back. You will be rightfully established from that day forward. Though it takes time, be patient with Him and just know that you are finally going in the right direction. Therefore, DO NOT let anyone cause you to turn around.

Share this daily WORD.

Mark 13:31
Heaven and earth shall pass away: but my words shall not pass away.

Word Wonders

Day Thirteen
Praise & Honor

Have you ever been in a store or somewhere, and saw disobedient children, sassing their parents or acting terrible? That is a sight I can not stand. The first thought comes to mind, is my children better not ever embarrass me like that or else. That is how many people treat God every day. They are sassy, cruel, ungrateful, and very disobedient. God wants us to be joyful as we praise, and honor Him. He does not want us to be resentful, but glad about Him, and His WORD. He doesn't want us to be frightened of His WORD, but fearful not to misrepresent His authority. I am not afraid of my mother, although I fear to upset her or to disrespecting her. I was not always a good child when I was young. But as I grew up and had children I gained a better respect for motherhood and my mother. All the trouble I caused when I was younger especially being a teenager. I regretted because she has only been good to me and no mother deserves to disrespect. So I learned to respect better my mom. Once we highly respect His commandments, He will be glad to bless us. Every day makes a considerable effort towards causing Him to be honored because he is my Heavenly Father.

My Daily Word

> *Psalms 112:1*
> *PRAISE ye the LORD. Blessed is the man that feareth the LORD, that delighted greatly in his commandments.*

This scripture is self explanatory. There is no secrets to being blessed, just take pleasure in His commandments. Many people search years for secrets on how to be blessed or gain good things. Just delight yourself in Him, and He will take pleasure in showing you great favor from on high.

Share this daily WORD.

Mark 13:31
Heaven and earth shall pass away: but my words shall not pass away.

Word Wonders

Day Fourteen
Kick Start Your Day

One day I was lying on the couch as my children were getting themselves ready for school. As I lay there, I saw a nice looking family helping their children prepare themselves for their day. Here I was lying on my couch being lazy because I was tired. Preparing your children for a caring attitude and love early in the morning is a good way to help nurture them to a good start for the day. I use to want my children to grow up, so they can become self-sufficient. But, for years, I had it all wrong. A good morning start, with a good breakfast and early morning inspirational words of encouragement will get them off to an incredible start. I realized, they still needed me to help kick start their day. Our children need us in more ways one. So enjoy their tender years, and instill as much love in them. Bright early in the morning gives them kind words of encouragement. Because one day you will wish you could prepare their breakfast, and they will be grown and out of the house.

My Daily Word

> *Psalms 112:2*
> *His seed shall be mighty upon the earth: the generation of the upright shall be blessed.*

I did not realize how powerful the word trust was until I came to believed in the WORD. Perhaps, I could have saved my family a whole lot of cursed days. Once we wake up and realize life is too valuable to waste, then we will start doing what is necessary to get ahead. I too had high hopes and dreams, but they were not happening. So, therefore, I fell in a slump because my hope had stopped. I realized that I was too close to stop, and my children needed for me to accomplish what I had stopped on. I wanted my children to be blessed, but it was all up to me to do what was right and all I needed to. I wanted them to inherit my blessings and not my debt, bills or curses. Do what you need to, so that your children will be blessed. The less you do now, the more you will put strains on their future. It is up to you to give them a head start in life. Let all your seeds be richly blessed, not cursed! Whatever you do today, matters tomorrow.

Share this daily WORD.

Mark 13:31
Heaven and earth shall pass away: but my words shall not pass away.

Word Wonders

Day Fifteen
Burst Through

I no longer want to be accountable for holding back someone's victory. Once you finish the work God has given you, someone freedom is your victory. Get to work, and remember faith without works are dead. If you have faith, then you will also show forth the works of your faith. Everyone will see your substance because even a seed must burst through the ground. What's bursting through your ground?

My Daily Word

Psalms 112:3
Wealth and riches shall be in his house: and his righteousness endureth for ever.

It is not all about money, but it is about your integrity. There are a lot of wealthy people with money, but no wisdom, goodness, righteousness and integrity. Your money does not size up your wealth, although your integrity will. Do not allow anyone, no situation, no circumstance or condition, to cause you to compromise your integrity. Let decency be a natural part of your everyday living and you will be richly blessed all the days of your life. And your seed will inherit your wealth. What do you want to leave behind?

Share this daily WORD.

Mark 13:31
Heaven and earth shall pass away: but my words shall not pass away.

Word Wonders

Day Sixteen
Destined

Prepare yourself daily with a new WORD along with a good morning prayer. He will counsel you through your daily tasks. It is not wise to go without instruction. If you do not get direction to a place that you have never been, then you will waste a lot of time and energy. For years, I wanted to go to a particular place, and I knew God had great things in store for me there. Often, I rushed without getting instruction, and direction. I was trying to get somewhere I have never been, but I was lost. All I had to do was to get proper leadership and follow through. Do not try and get there by yourself, because He may have somewhere different in mind. Furthermore, stop wasting time; know where you are destined to be in life.

My Daily Word

> *Psalms 119:133*
> *Order my steps in thy word and let not any iniquity have dominion over me.*

Many people allow their sins to stop them from furthering in the WORD. One thing I can say about King David, he did not let any iniquity stop him from praising God. After all, David was the apple of God's eye. Sin is purposed to interrupt righteousness from going in effect in our lives. Do not let it stop you from allowing the WORD from ordering your steps. Give into the WORD and let the WORD have dominion over your life, not sin! Hasn't sin stolen enough from you? Do not give it anymore of your time, because your time is too valuable to waste. Life is a terrible thing to waste!

Share this daily WORD.

Mark 13:31
Heaven and earth shall pass away: but my words shall not pass away.

Word Wonders

Day Seventeen
Receive Instructions

One thing you must comprehend is how to receive instruction. If you like to do things the hard way or perhaps your way, then continue to suffer. Nevertheless, if you want to do things the right way then let the WORD show you how. I know you have experienced buying something that you had to put together. The directions suck; especially if you already know where all the parts go. Once you get it all together, you have a lot of extra pieces left over. Just because it looks like you are finished, it will not last. There was a lot of missing pieces you forgot to include. Well, that is an excellent example of many lives today. Just as they think they have it together, their lives will fall apart, and then they have to start all over. It is best to do things right the first time.

My Daily Word

Psalms 119:105
Thy word is a lamp unto my feet, and a light unto my path.

Many days I did not know where I was going, but the WORD guided me. When I could not see for myself, the WORD was my sight. Let the WORD be the light to your feet, as the WORD steers you into the right path of life.

Share this daily WORD.

Mark 13:31
Heaven and earth shall pass away: but my words shall not pass away.

Word Wonders

Day Eighteen
Don't Fail Yourself

Often we complicate our life, by not getting things right the first time around. One night I was talking to my son. I was explaining his grades must improve because he will only hurt himself. As the next year rolls around, he will find himself repeating the same grade over, if he does not get it right. As adults, we are just like our children in school. We fail ourselves, our family, our goals and our dreams. Also, year after year we try to accomplish something, by doing the same old thing. Again we fail, by simply not doing things the right way. For once in your life, make up your mind to do it the right way and finish what you started. If you had done the right thing the first time, you would not be where you are right now. Finish what you started and do not let anything or anyone interrupts you this time around.

My Daily Word

Psalms 119:130
The entrance of thy words giveth light; it giveth understanding unto the simple.

It is time to prove to yourself that you want a better way of living, by inviting the WORD into your life. Let The WORD enter your heart and apply it to your everyday life. Once I received the truth in my life, things were not as hard as I thought. I was no longer walking blindly because The WORD was my guide. Let The WORD enter and stop avoiding it, you are only shunning away your favor from The Most High.

Share this daily WORD.

Mark 13:31
Heaven and earth shall pass away: but my words shall not pass away.

Word Wonders

Day Nineteen
Make Your Request Known

God wants you to ask Him for things, which is what the scripture says (Philippians 6:12). Make your request known, just ask Him. Many have said do not ask God because He knows what you want. Well, if you want it, ask Him. He has all your needs, wants and desires. Plus, He has the power to give them to you. As you inquire about things, that gives Him the opportunity to work on you. He loves it when He can reconstruct a new you for others to see. Yes, life will throw many curve balls our way, and get us completely off track, and out of line with Gods will. First of all, He wants you to be able to handle what you are praying. So, therefore, He may have to do some inner work on you to get you prepared for what you are expecting of Him. You may not know when or how just know He is going to answer you. Make your request known to your Way Maker, and be patient as you wait. If you had some beautiful furnishings, and now you are planning to remodel would you give it to someone that will not appreciate, or take care of it? Absolutely, not! Well, that is how God is when we ask Him for stuff. He gives it to us when we are ready to take care of our blessings. Otherwise, He would not receive glory. When God's glory can be revealed to you, then you will be ready for all of your prayers to be answered, and not just a few. My question to you is, are you ready? If you answered yes, then get dress because your time is here!

My Daily Word

Philippians 6:12
Becareful for nothing and supplication with thanksgiving
let your requests be made known unto God.

Your better be careful what you are praying for, because their will be a pattern of responsibility that is required. The more you pray is the more you are seeking to gain wisdom. Surely, He will give it all to you, but are you willing to do what He requires of you? Nothing is for free, there will be a sacrifice. Many things I asked Him for and I paid a dear sacrifice before I received it. Through the years as He answered my prayers my family and friends also paid a dear price . I was not perfect and I made a lot of mistakes, but I did a hefty price as they saw me going through. God will not give you something that you are not prepared to handle. So be careful as you pray, He will give it to you but be prepare to endure what you must in order to get it. What ever you do, hold on and do not quit because it is not worth it.

Share this daily WORD.

Mark 13:31
Heaven and earth shall pass away: but my words shall not pass away.

Word Wonders

Day Twenty
Togetherness Matters

God wants to work with you. If you stand with Him, you will receive power, and if you stand for Him, He will abide in you. Jesus wants you as His business partner. You take care of His business, and He will take care of your business. It is time to be about your father's business because Jesus is tired of you loosing. He has a heavenly fortune waiting on you now. Things not made by man hands and doors opened that no man has the power to shut.

My Daily Word

> John 15:7
> *If ye abide in me, and my words abide in you, ye shall ask what you will, and it shall be done unto you.*

God does not mind answering prayers. He loves it. Nevertheless, He does not like to be used or taken for granted. However, He truly blesses those that take the time to stand on His Word, and with Him. Wouldn't you help those more that stood by your side? The ones that abide by Him, and bear His WORD will have his obligation to answer their request. You must be in Him, get inside The WORD, and The Word will get inside you.

Share this daily WORD.

Mark 13:31
Heaven and earth shall pass away: but my words shall not pass away.

Ponder on This WORD

James 1:12
Blessed is the man that endureth temptation: for when he is tried, he shall receive the crown of life, which the LORD hath promised to them that love him.

Every time we do not give into temptation, we become more powerful. Temptations only exist to cause our minds to stay in a position of poverty. Temptations only ruin lives, dreams, families and it will destroy your hope. It is the number one identity theft, and it incriminates your character. The temptation is potent, only if you give in. It has the power to destroy your life. Every time you face temptation, look in the mirror and convince yourself that you are better than that.

Once many give into temptation, they give up on their blessing and forfeit on their promises. Most promises come with a stipulation, and it is only good if you keep your part of the bargain. Do not bargain with your future; it is not worth it. Because it is not only your life, but it is everyone that is connected to you. I have seen a lot of people swindle downward because of temptation, and they lost everything they had. A temptation of the flesh is incredibly powerful, and it has ruined many lives even the most articulate and it has no respect for a person. It will devour whosoever is willing to give in. That is a lot of blood on one's hands, so be careful and stay prayed up.

One scripture, in particular, helped me through temptation when I quit smoking, James 4:7. Many days I quoted this scripture as temptation was all around me, and the more I resisted the enemy, the more he fled. And furthermore, remove yourself away from temptation and anyone or anything that brings temptation around. When you put it in your mind to quit something, you must leave all behind especially if you are serious. It is your soul that you are protecting, surely your soul is worth it. The more you resist, the more power you will gain. It is hard to do it alone. So, therefore, do it with The WORD.

Word Wonders

Day Twenty One
Be Grateful

Sometimes our heart can not help, but to be troubled. It seems that trouble appears everywhere you go, but you must get a grip on life. Some things in life are more powerful, and will stress you out. Let it go and let God take care of the things that were out of my control. As He delivers you, stay out, and be obedient to His voice. Remember, do not take listening to the voice of God for granted, because there was a time you could not hear Him. Be grateful that He is even speaking to you, and listening.

My Daily Word

> *John 14:1*
> *LET not your heart be troubled: ye believe in God, believe also in me.*

Every time you worry about your troubles, you forbid God to handle them. Let God be God, He knows His duty better than you. Permit Him to take care of your troubles daily, and do not try to handle what is bigger than you. Let Him handle your troubles, which is the best advice I can give you. Once you hire a moving company you do not try to lift your belongings yourself. You let them do it. So therefore once you pray about your troubles, leave the troubles with God. Let Him move them out of your way. When you trust in the WORD, it will work amazing things out for you. The WORD is my Miracle Worker and couldn't image my life without it. When my trials overwhelmed me, the WORD sustained me.

Share this daily WORD.

Isaiah 55:11

So shall my word be that goeth forth out of my mouth: it shall not return unto me void, but it shall accomplish that which I please, and it shall prosper in the thing whereto I sent it.

Word Wonders

Day Twenty Two
When You Are Being Stripped

One day I did not have all the things I use to. My life had taken a spiral down, and I was stripped of everything I had worked so hard for. I mean a hardcore fall. My life just wasn't what it used to be. I had no money and no savings. All I had was the WORD, and all my bills were past due. At that time, I was facing the court for eviction and had recently lost all of my vehicles. I had to send out a WORD, which is all I had. Remember; I was once a Co-Pastor, a leader in the church, and a preacher of the gospel. I had taught many series on faith, and trust. I was left with nothing, but the WORD! I needed a way out. God showed up in my life, just when I thought that everything was all over. The WORD was my income, my stability, and it gave me the ability to gain again. It caused me to become able to stand when I had lost my hope. It picked me up and placed my feet on a solid ROCK. Now I am able, and all it took was a small portion of the WORD. I told the Lord that you were going to be my helper because the Bible tells me so. Plus Jesus said, "Heaven and earth will pass away, but the WORD will never fell me." So, therefore, I expect Jesus to help me in my helpless situations, after all, that is what His WORD says. I let the WORD work for me, and it did! The WORD is always at work for me even when I can't. When you can't see your way, let the WORD be your way maker. It will be your legs and stand, your eyes to see and your hands when you can not help yourself.

My Daily Word

Luke 21:33
Heaven and earth shall pass away: but my words shall not pass away.

Daily assign a WORD to go out before you, put the WORD to work in your life. The WORD is where your power is. Do not put your trust into worldly things and possessions, but in the WORD. The WORD will produce just what it says it will and do what you send it out to do. It will not come back unto your void, unless your faith is not there. You may fail you, but the WORD will never fail you. Put all the trust into the WORD, and it will not fail you.

Share this daily WORD.

Isaiah 55:11
So shall my word be that goeth forth out of my mouth: it shall not return unto me void, but it shall accomplish that which I please, and it shall prosper in the thing whereto I sent it.

Word Wonders

Day Twenty Three
Take the Limits Off

Some people put limits on what they can ask God. Take the limits off, because He can give you more than what you ask of Him. Haven't He proved Himself to you already? There are plenty of things you currently have that you did not ask for, but He gave them to you anyway. He is able! Ask what you want, and watch how He gives it to you. Sometimes, once we ask God for things, we do not always know how He is going to give us things. Often He may allow you to go through another trial before He gives it to you. Much is given, much is required. Many of us have to mature into a more responsible person and be more spiritually developed before He gives us our request. If you had a twelve-year-old son, and he asked to drive your car, would you let him? No. He knows, and you know that he would have to be educated to drive. There are school courses that come before he can receive his driver's license. Surely one day after he is old enough you will let him drive your car, but it will come later in life. That is the same with us, some things we must be educated on before he answers our request. Be patient, it will come to pass. Although there is a time for everything, He will answer you. Just be patient, mature and prepare yourself while you are waiting.

My Daily Word

> *1 John 5:15*
> *And if we know that he hear us, whatsoever we ask, we know that we have the petitions that we desired of Him.*

God will give you what you ask of Him, but you must be patient while you are waiting. You can ask Him whatever you want, once you come to know Him. Because you will know that, the answer will be yes. Nothing is too big or too small for God; He is all-powerful.

Share this daily WORD.

Isaiah 55:11
So shall my word be that goeth forth out of my mouth: it shall not return unto me void, but it shall accomplish that which I please, and it shall prosper in the thing whereto I sent it.

Word Wonders

Day Twenty Four
All Powerful

If it had not been for the Lord on my side, I do not know where I would be? Jesus had been my DELIVERER even when I did not know Him. He took great care of me, even when I was not considering His ways. Eventually, I had to put His WORD first. It was never meant to be easy trying to choose the right the wrong. He gives liberty to us all, and the choice is ours to make. It is up to you, who you will serve and trust. One day I just chose to walk in the WORD and to respect His ways. The WORD that works in you gives you power, just let it work.

My Daily Word

Isaiah 50:10
Who is among you that feareth the LORD, that obeyeth the voice of his servant, that walketh in darkness, and hath no light? Let him trust in the name of the LORD, and stay upon his God.

He has allowed you to get to this point in your life. Now He wants you to walk in the light. Plus, as He delivers you He wants you to stay in Him. Begin to daily meditate on His goodness that He offers and promise us. No one will be able to do all that He can for you, so why turn away from the one that loves you the most? If He took care of you while you walked in darkness. What more would He be willing to do for you as you be obedient? Everything that you could ever ask of Him will be given to you, trust in Him and He will build your confidence in Him.

Share this daily WORD.

Isaiah 55:11
So shall my word be that goeth forth out of my mouth: it shall not return unto me void, but it shall accomplish that which I please, and it shall prosper in the thing whereto I sent it.

Word Wonders

Day Twenty Five
The Choice Is Yours

Often we do not realize how our lives are affecting others around us. It is hard trying, but it will be easier when you do what is right. Someone is watching you. They are noticing your every move, and your moves may be incriminating their trust in God. Remember someone is watching you. Once God begins His work on you, it is not okay for you to hang in the same areas or around the same people unless they are walking in agreement with walking worthy. Because as long as you straddle the fence, the longer it is going to take for your blessing. What do you want more curses or blessing, the choice is yours?

My Daily Word

> *Psalms 1:1*
> *BLESSED is the man that walketh not in the counsel of the ungodly, nor standeth in the way of sinners, nor sitteth in the seat of the scornful.*

I became careful whose seat I set in, and who I was around. We must be careful of our close association; they may not be living righteous, and it could rub off on you. It is noble not to follow the crowd, and not to go where they go. Despise sin, and know that it is impossible for you to serve two masters at once. Let others boldly know who you rightfully serve, and do not be ashamed of Jesus. Remember, do not get in the way of sinners, sit with them or associate with them. Now, this does not mean that you can not be a blessing to them when they may need you. They need you to share the WORD with them, love and hope. People who are walking unworthy need to see the righteous do what is right. We must be a living example, not straddling the fence. Cause someone to reach out for Jesus by the way you live. Remember, and somebody is watching you. Your life will either promote Jesus or demote Jesus, which one do you prefer because your life is representing.

Share this daily WORD.

Isaiah 55:11
So shall my word be that goeth forth out of my mouth: it shall not return unto me void, but it shall accomplish that which I please, and it shall prosper in the thing whereto I sent it.

Word Wonders

Day Twenty Six
Unimaginable

Searching the WORD for power is your manifestation source. Anytime you are ready to multiply, and become fruitful; you will get in the WORD. Soak your mind, heart, and soul daily in the WORD. The more you meditate on the WORD is, the less power the enemies will have over your life. Forbid them entrance into your mind, body, soul and heart. Where ever the word is, there is life, and there is no room for the enemy. Plus, the truth which is the WORD shall set you free. Exchange some of your extracurricular time, and activities in for the WORD, and meditate on it. You will inherit an incredible blessing, multiply greatly and gain peace surpass all understanding. Manifestation will be your evidence that your faith brought unimaginable substance.

My Daily Word

Psalms 1:2
But his delight is in the law of the LORD; and in his law doth he meditate day and night.

The WORD is the law. God wants us to meditate day and night on His WORD. As we share it with others, we are meditating. As we testify, and study we are meditating. In addition, as we read the WORD, pray the WORD, speak the WORD we are meditating on His goodness. The WORD is good and it gives life. The more you meditate on the WORD is the more powerful you will operate through and in the WORD.

Share this daily WORD.

Isaiah 55:11

So shall my word be that goeth forth out of my mouth: it shall not return unto me void, but it shall accomplish that which I please, and it shall prosper in the thing whereto I sent it.

Word Wonders

Day Twenty Seven
Make Him Tremble & Fall

When trouble comes, the enemies are trying to stop you from entering into your season. What the enemy does not understand is that nothing can stop your season when you are a genuine faith walker! Not even God can hold this period because this season was already predestined to come. Seasons come in four different climates such as summer, fall, spring, and winter. There is springing forth season, falling off season, summer time fun season, and a winter hibernating season. When your season comes, you will begin to prosper without cause. It will even amaze you how blessed you are. When it is your season, it is just your time. As you look on the calendar, you will know there is a seasonal change that must take place. Just look at your life, and know that your personal seasonal change is here. Trouble does not last always, and joy is coming keep your hope thriving on a fresh word, speak it aloud and see transformation right before your eyes. Satan might not fear your words but the WORD of the Lord and at the name of JESUS - Satan trembles. Make him tremble and stand up in Jesus name.

My Daily Word

> *Psalms 1:3*
> *And he shall be like a tree planted by the rivers of water, that bringeth forth his fruit in is season; his leaf also shall not wither; and whatsoever he doeth shall prosper.*

This is to the exact point God wants to bring all His children. To be able to gain prosperity in a manner that whatever they put their minds to do will prosper. He brought me to a place in life that I was not prepared to give up all I had worked so hard for, just the power to be able to stand on His WORD. Once you come into that power to stand, you will not be moved because you will be rooted in the word. The WORD is your ground and everything you will put your hands to do that is good, will bring forth fruit. You work, and your endurance will not wither, but become replenished as well as prosper. Nothing will be able to stop you in your season.

Share this daily WORD.

Isaiah 55:11
So shall my word be that goeth forth out of my mouth: it shall not return unto me void, but it shall accomplish that which I please, and it shall prosper in the thing whereto I sent it.

Word Wonders

Day Twenty Eight
Milk & Honey

Building a bond with God through getting to know Him in the WORD will create in you a new confidence. Plus, confidence gives you power. It is beautiful when you show great respect towards others, and it is more powerful as you do the same for the WORD. Give God want He wants, compliance, and honor. Go back, and follow all that He commands you well as His commandments. Your promise land flowing with milk and honey is waiting for you, but you must walk at His command with compliance.

My Daily Word

Psalms 119:48
My hands also will I lift unto thy commandments, which I have loved; and I will meditate in thy statutes.

Include the WORD time in your day, and make time to meditate on the WORD. Getting to know Him is the key to gaining power. Once He commands you to do something just do it, to the best of your ability, which is what He loves. You satisfy Him and watch how good your return be. The more satisfaction you give Him is the more satisfaction you will receive.

Share this daily WORD.

Isaiah 55:11
So shall my word be that goeth forth out of my mouth: it shall not return unto me void, but it shall accomplish that which I please, and it shall prosper in the thing whereto I sent it.

Word Wonders

Day Twenty Nine
Be Bold

There are many working in the field for Him, and they are bringing Him shame. He does not need one more shameful worker helping the enemy out. He needs soldiers that are prepared to stand on the WORD and standing BOLD on His WORD. He needs us to speak the truth and live truthfully at all times. Can God depend on you to cause Him to reap more glory?

My Daily Word

II Timothy 2:15
Study to shew thyself approved unto God, a workman that needeth not to be ashamed, rightly divided the word of truth.

He is going to hold all of us responsible for seeking truth for ourselves. You must spend quality time in and with the WORD. Study for yourself and do not go on what others tell you or teach or preach to you. Get to know the WORD for yourself. He needs bold workers working for the KINGDOM not those that do not have a clue as to who He is.

Share this daily WORD.

Isaiah 55:11
So shall my word be that goeth forth out of my mouth: it shall not return unto me void, but it shall accomplish that which I please, and it shall prosper in the thing whereto I sent it.

Word Wonders

Day Thirty
Pray Your Way Out

I know it is a scary thing when you do not know which way life is taking you. If no one else knows, I do. It still brings tears to my eyes when I went through a stormy season that lasted for years. It seems as though it wasn't going never to end. It lasted for years, and it was incarcerating. I almost lost my mind. Do not set your eyes on the storms in your life, nor attention to those terrible trials. They have taken enough from you. Do not give up your joy. Do not look at them, just bow down, and pray. Dissecting the problem is not going to work either, but prayer will. Bow down, and be grateful for the opportunity that the storm did not kill you. It may have taken your possessions, friends, or someone you love dearly. Nevertheless, be grateful you are still here. Someone needs you to overcome and to make it out alive. Take all your burdens, and troubles to God; just cast all your cares on Him. Kneel as often as needed for this storm is going to take serious prayer power. Pray your way out.

My Daily Word

Proverbs 3:5
Trust in the Lord with all tine heart; and lean not unto thine own understanding.

We can only lean on the WORD when we can not comprehend what is going on in our life. Not all things are for us to understand right away, but as time shall pass they will reveal. God works in ways that are mysterious to men but be grateful that He is at work in your life. Many times things may not appear to be going right, but He is still working it out just for you. Trust in the Lord; because He will never fail you nor forsake you. (Hebrew 13:6)

Share this daily WORD.

Isaiah 55:11
So shall my word be that goeth forth out of my mouth: it shall not return unto me void, but it shall accomplish that which I please, and it shall prosper in the thing whereto I sent it.

Word Wonders

Day Thirty One
Are You Saved?

One evening my children, and I was sitting at the dinner table. I asked them the question. Are you saved? They answered, yes. And I asked, "How do you know that you are saved?" They gave me every answer but the right one. And, after dinner, we discussed the truth. It is valuable to have private Bible lessons at home with your family because ministry begins at home.

My Daily Word

Romans 10:9
That if thou shalt confess with thy mouth the Lord Jesus, and shalt believe in thine heart that God hath raised him from the dead, thou shalt be saved.

Ask yourself this question, are you saved? It is a simple process. Confess with your mouth that Jesus is Lord and believe in your heart that God raised His son from the dead. After, following those simple directions, now you are saved. Share this scripture with others and have them to repeat what this scripture says. Also, read Romans 8-12 and enjoy freedom in Jesus.

Share this daily WORD.

Isaiah 55:11
So shall my word be that goeth forth out of my mouth: it shall not return unto me void, but it shall accomplish that which I please, and it shall prosper in the thing whereto I sent it.

Word Wonders

Thanks For Your Support
&

I pray that Word Wonders blessed your life to inspire you to live righteous and for The Most High to cause favor to appear in your life – like never before. Thanks for choosing another Anointed book by Parice Parker, please indulge yourself in another.

Remember, Let Your Hope Influence Your Faith.

~ Parice Parker

Word Wonders

What inspired me to write this book?

One day my neighbor came over and brought my book, "Living Life In A Messed Up Situation." She said, "this book is so powerful andI passed it around to my friends, family, and neighbors. Do you have any devotional books? I don't like to read, but yours kept my attention." At the time, I did not have any daily devotional books. So I wrote Word Wonders in the request from a friendly neighbor. I was very sick during that period, and writing truly helps me heal. It's like medicine, and this book was my healing power after having a stroke. I struggle to write because my thoughts were scrambled, but the Lord gave me all the words to say in Word Wonders. I listened to need, disciplined myself to write and birth a book. If you listen you will be amazed, all He will birth through your obedience.

Authentically Made,
Apostle, Parice Parker

Ephesians 3:7, Whereof I was made a minister,
According to the gift of the grace of God
given unto me by the effectual working of
his power.

Dedications to the special people in my life:

All that was present in my life during hard times and remained, showing love.

My heart says,

"thank you and I pray each gets sweeter and better just for you!"

Empower Your Daily Thoughts

Other Inspirational Books by Parice Parker

- _Living Life in A Messed Up Situation_

  Volume One

- _Living Life in A Messed Up Situation_

  Volume Two

- _A Precious Gift from God_

- _The Anointing Powers of Your Hands_

- _Word Wonders_

- _The Birth of an Author Shall Be Born_

- _From Eating Crumbs to Transforming Life_

- _Live Laugh Love & Be Happy_

- _Breaking the Back of Poverty (Book)_

- _Breaking the Back of Poverty (Journal)_

- _Power to Push You_

Empower Your Daily Thoughts

To Order Inspirational Books by Parice Parker please visit
her online bookstore www.pariceparker.biz

CEO of Fountain of Life Publisher's House

The House of Transformation Miracle Ministries or Fountain
of Life Empowerment Ministries

Please Mail All Correspondence

To: P. O Box 922612 Norcross GA 30010

Attention: Apostle Parice Parker

Aggravated Assault On Your Mind

Phenomenal: Have you ever felt, the very person you have surely loved or believed in has attacked you? It may have been your closest friend, relative, child, your spouse or even yourself. Sometimes you wanted to cry and could not. Shortly afterwards, while gazing about the pain immediately tears began to fall as a flowing river. Your heart has been assaulted and snared with claws of intentions to kill. A multitude of thoughts circulate in your mind and then you began to say to yourself **"How did I let this happen to me?"** Your situation was bound to occur, because somewhere along the way you have allowed your circumstance to control your mind. Allegedly, you put your trust in the wrong one or thing and then you are thrown off guard. Most definitely, you wonder, who do I blame? You did not realize you have entrusted so much of your heart to be assaulted through the passion of love you have given. A since of blindness has overwhelmed your thinking ability, rearranging your life, and throwing it off balance. Truly, there is an explanation and an apology due, but none is ever given. Certainly, you have tried to generate an effectual change. Perhaps, the more you have tried, the more your relationship seemed to die. **Instantly thinking, What Is The Use?**

A Precious Gift from God

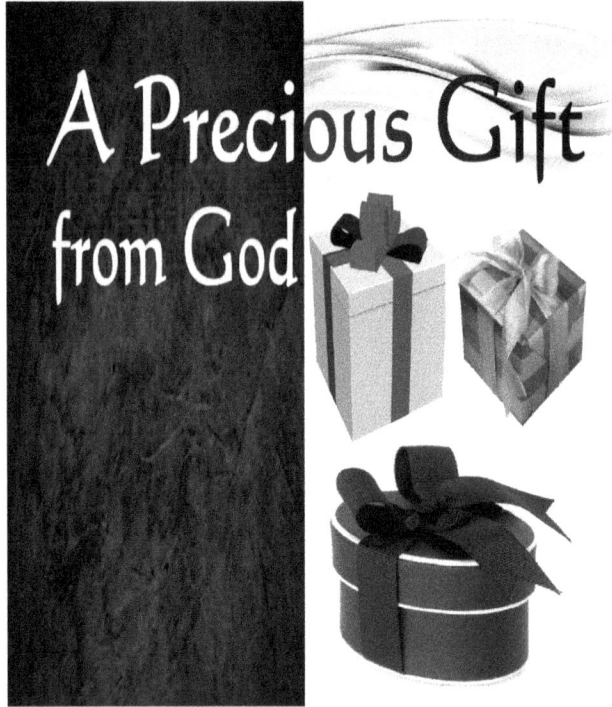

Talent Is Too Good To Waste

Parice C Parker

Your Gift Discovery? It teaches one the value of their natural born talent and motivates one to Live Life On Purpose! This book inspires the heart, gives courage to your *How to Ability* and causes you to live in the pursuit of your happiness. Every natural born leader needs to read this book, it is **AWE – INSPIRING!**

Living Life In A Messed Up Situation
Volume One

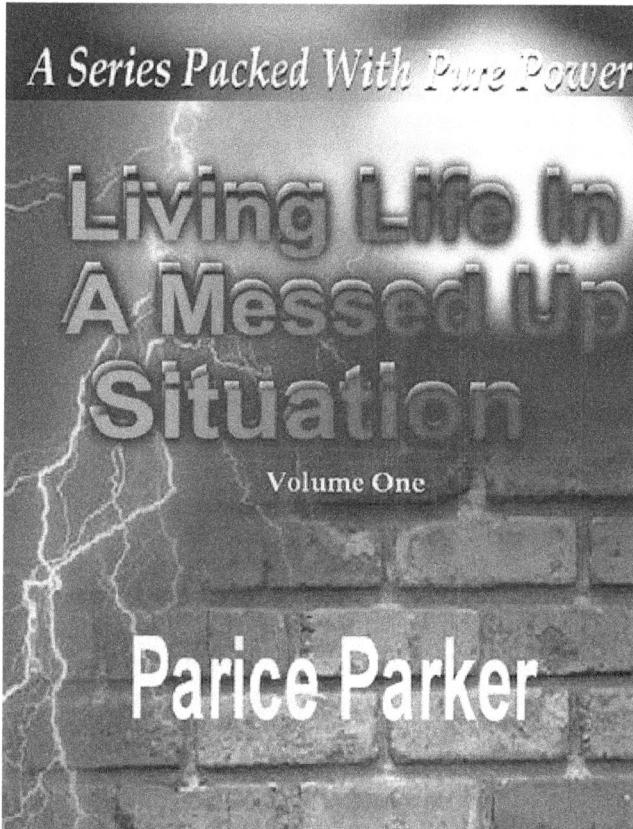

Powerful: God will assign the most in-depth spiritual cleaning service through the Blood of Jesus the Christ to clean up your messed up life. **Every messed up situation that you are living** in will have a **Sparkling Effect** when God gets finished with you. Some things He dusts off, others He wipes down and some need to be polished to shine. **Get Polished Perfect** after reading this book and simply gain it all.

The Birth of An Author Shall Be Born

The Birth
of an Author
Shall Be
Born
Is it you?

- Overcome writer's block
- Motivation to write
- Placing your chapters's
- Finding time to write
- How to begin your book
- Staying focus & more ...

"Secrets to Mastering Book Writing"
Parice Parker

Fascinating ... Dazing at the fact you have a book inside and don't know where to start or how to get it out! This book have dynamic key points and great strategies on how to succeed in book writing from start to finish. It's time to discover the author in you and to **GET THAT BOOK OUT Of YOU!** This book is full of techniques to motivate the author inside... The Birth of an Author Shall Be Born, Is It YOU?

Word Wonders

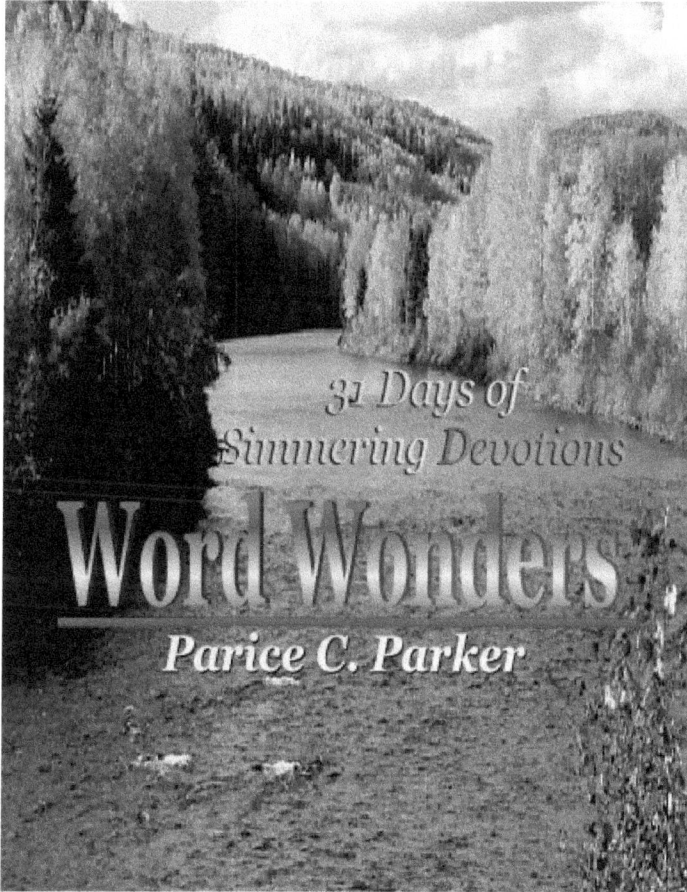

A Eye – Opening ... Word Wonder inspires your HOPE to Greatly Influence your FAITH and it's a magnificent daily devotional book to help keep you focused in word. It EMPOWERS Positive Powers to cause DIVINE FAVOR to ABOUND TOWARDS YOU! Simple things you need to be equipped with more favor from on high. Get This Book TODAY!

From Eating Crumbs To Transforming Wealth

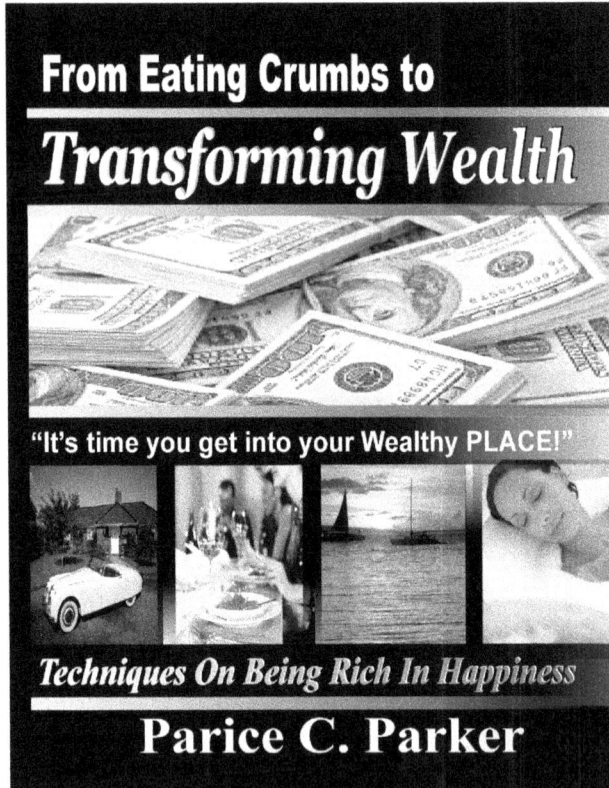

From Eating Crumbs to

Transforming Wealth

"It's time you get into your Wealthy PLACE!"

Techniques On Being Rich In Happiness

Parice C. Parker

Riveting … Finally, a book that keeps you in a thriving mental state that causes your HOPE to burst through! Now, it is time to identify the real you by introducing the TROPHY that is Hidden inside. It's your time to stop eating the crumbs of life and Indulge In Your WEALTHY Place!

The Anointing Powers of Your Hands

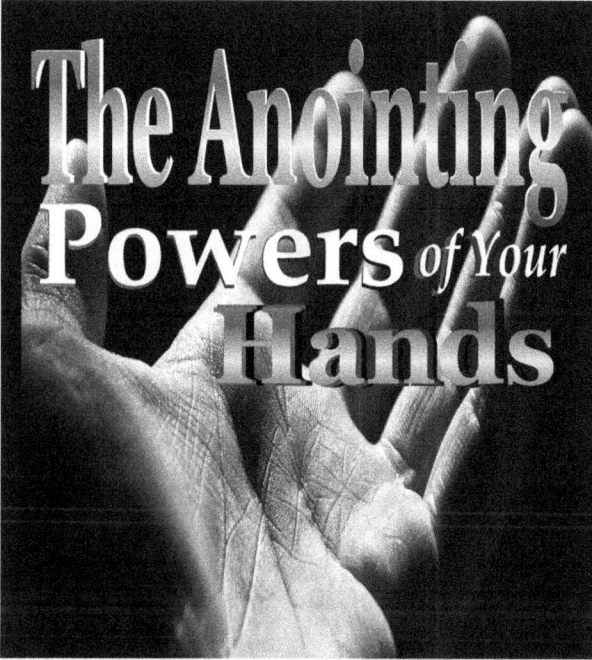

Do It, Doing It! Now, It's DONE! ...

Parice C. Parker

*Absorbing ...*The Anointing Powers of Your Hands has the ability to cause you to *REACH* for Dreams even You Thought They Were Impossible! It Motivates that **IMPOSSIBLE VISION TO COME TO PASS** and it places it in your **Rear View Mirror!**

Power to Push You

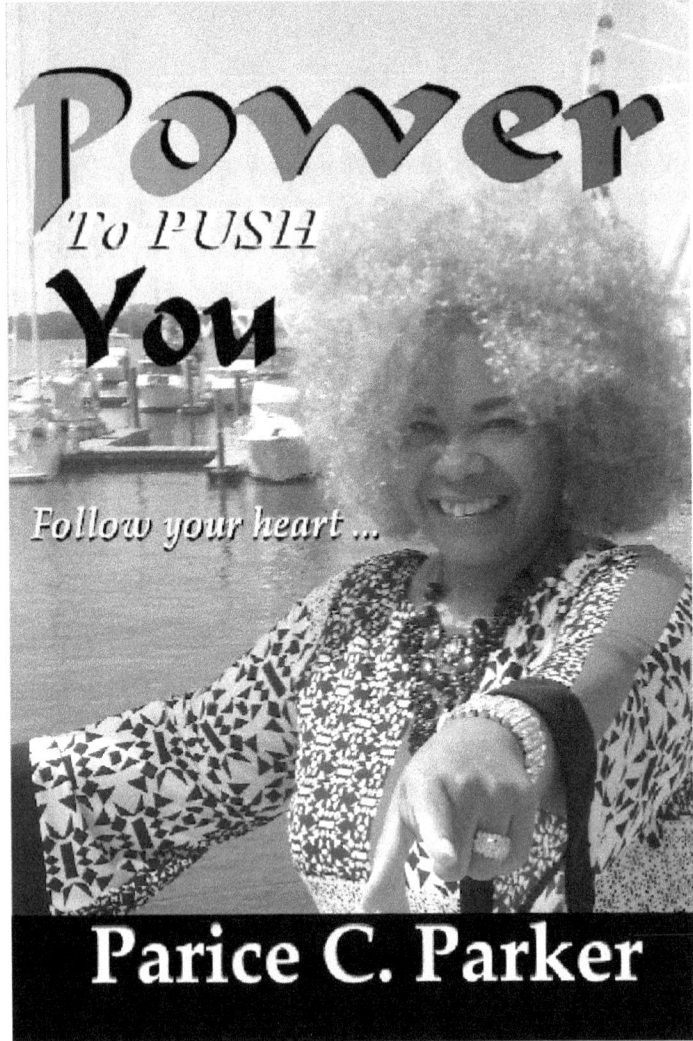

Military Force ... When you fix your mind on the power to excel and purpose to hit the target, then it is a done deal. Your goal is now to achieve. No one, nothing or tiredness could stop you now.

Power to Push You is missioned to cause you to be an eye specialist. Your eyes will begin to see the benefits of vision; the aspirations once accomplished, and you will have an **IMPEMTUOUS ZEAL.** No one can dream for this vision as you or push it in the manner you can and stay focused as you. Vision is the power to drive people but first one must see the fullness, must feel the passion for it to live and have an **IMPEMTUOUS ZEAL** to birth it. Vision is a life modifier and life decorator. It can give you a complete makeover from inside out. Also, when others see it, they will want to be a part or some of what you have. Your success will cause others to desire a much better life and give others a fresh hope to accomplish. Power to Push You speaks for itself and all that connects and read Power to Push You shall cause their visions to exist. It's a **DYNOMITE PUSHER!**

Live Love Laugh & Be Happy

It's like medicine to your bones ...

Parice Parker

Live Love Laugh & Be Happy *Fabulous* ... Daily many live life being terribly unhappy wanting others to really care but, are too often overlooked. It's time you get a new ray of hope. A time for healing inside and out. Live Love Laugh & Be Happy is purposed to expose new life to your everyday living. Your laughter is on its way, because those that sow in tears of sorrow, shall reap in tears of joy!

Fountain of Life Publishers House

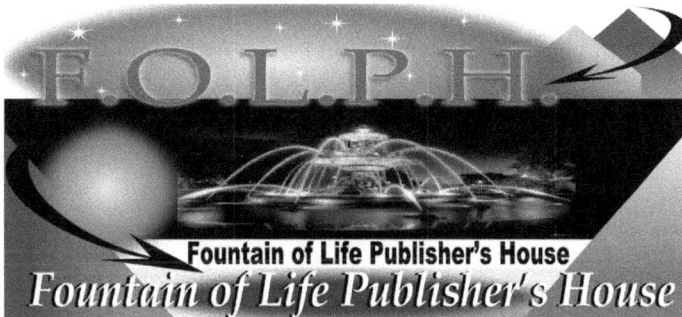

P. O. Box 922612, Norcross, GA 30010
Phone: 404.936.3989

For book orders or wholesale distribution
Website: www.pariceparker.biz

9 7